THE STORM MONSTER

by Lael Littke

illustrated by
Craig McFarland Brown

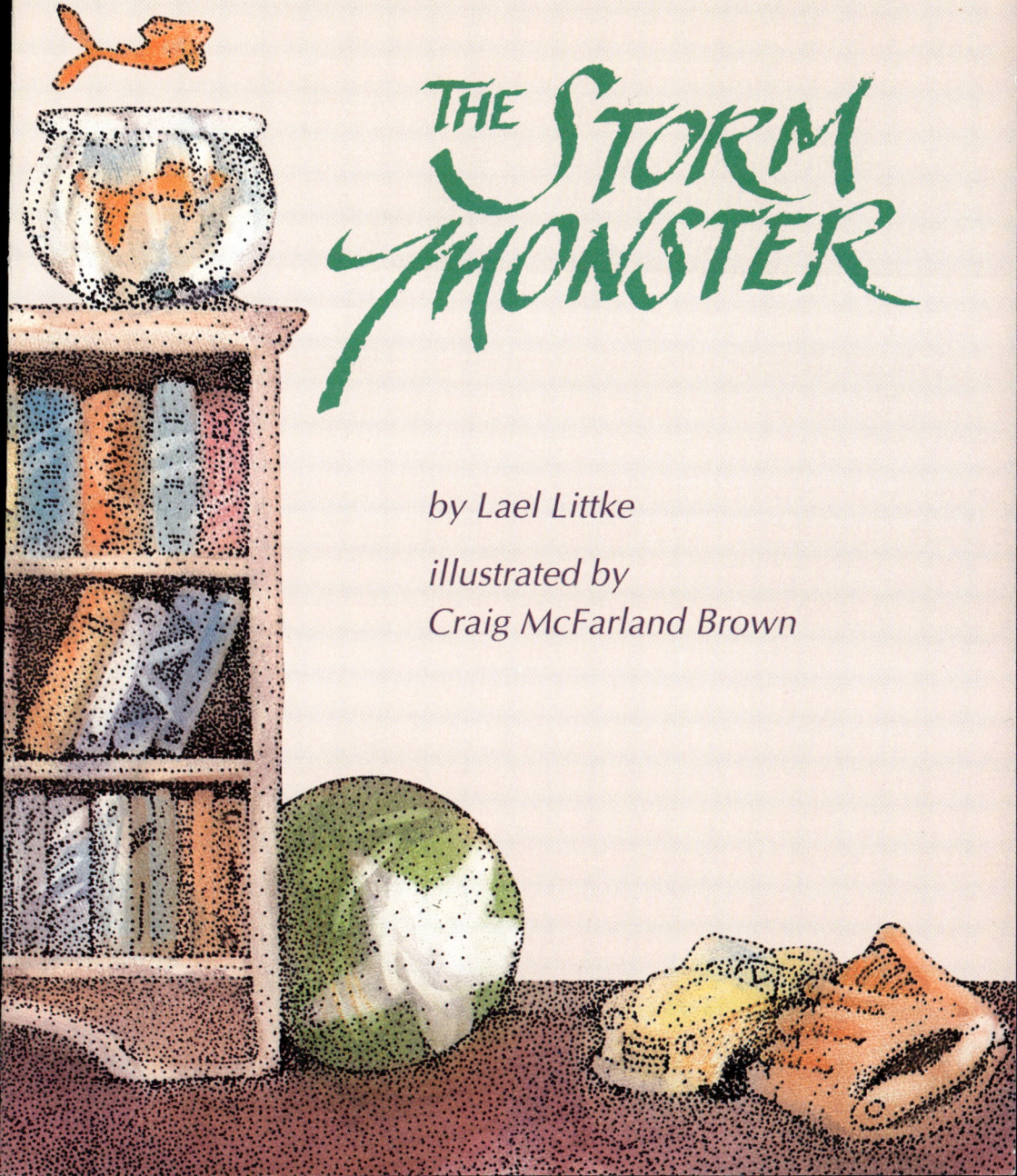

S I L V E R   B U R D E T T   &   G I N N

Simon & Schuster A Paramount Communications Company

Text © 1991 Silver, Burdett & Ginn Inc.
Art © 1991 Craig McFarland Brown.

ISBN 0-663-52960-3

Developed by Cebulash Associates

2   3   4   5   6   7   8   9   10   BA   95   94   93   92

The storm monster comes
with a terrible whoosh.

It rattles our door
with its hoosh and its shoosh.

I'm not scared, Waldo. Are you?

The storm monster hangs
like a ghost in our tree.
It blows at our house, at you and at me.

I'm not scared, Waldo. Are you?

The storm monster
flashes a light in my eye.

It rumbles and tumbles
across the whole sky.

It crashes and smashes as it passes by.

I'm scared, Waldo. Are you?

Now the monster is tapping
at our windowpane. It patters.
It spatters. Oh look, it's just rain.

I'm not scared, Waldo. Are you?

The storm monster leaves
in the wink of an eye.

Fly away, monster,
up to the sky.

I wasn't scared, Waldo.
Were you?